Bacharach & David

AMERICAN CLASSICS

ISBN 0-634-01148-0

HAL•LEONARD®
CORPORATION

7777 W. BLUEMOUND RD. P.O. BOX 13819 MILWAUKEE, WI 53213

Visit Hal Leonard Online at
www.halleonard.com

CONTENTS

ALFIE
Theme from the Paramount Picture ALFIE

Words by HAL DAVID
Music by BURT BACHARACH

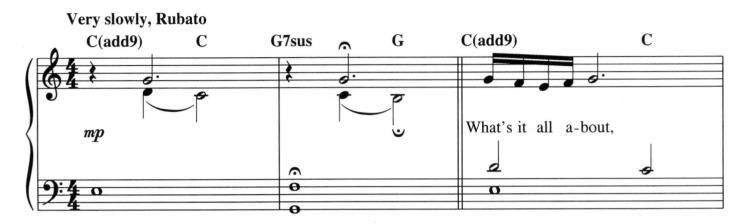

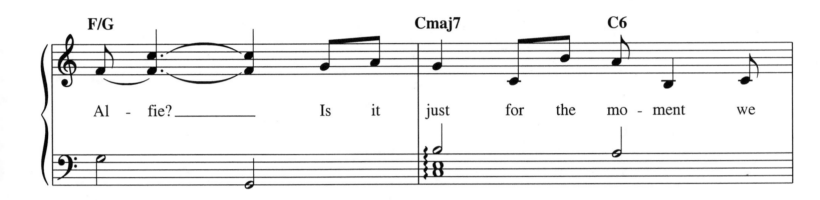

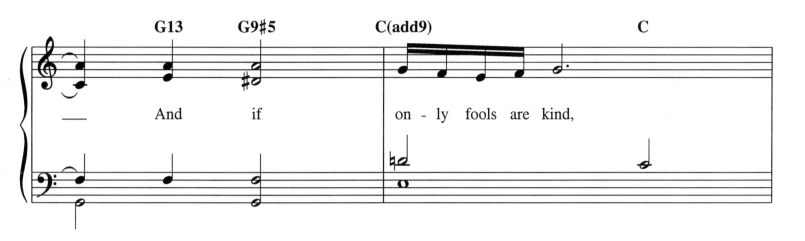

G13   G9#5   C(add9)   C

And if on - ly fools are kind,

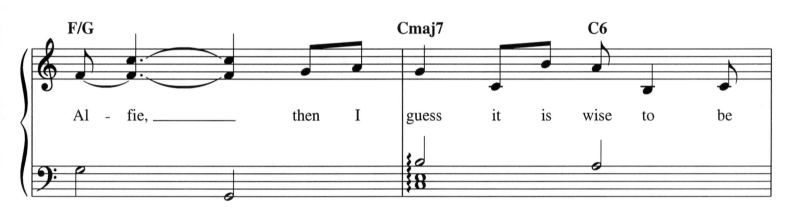

F/G   Cmaj7   C6

Al - fie, _____ then I guess it is wise to be

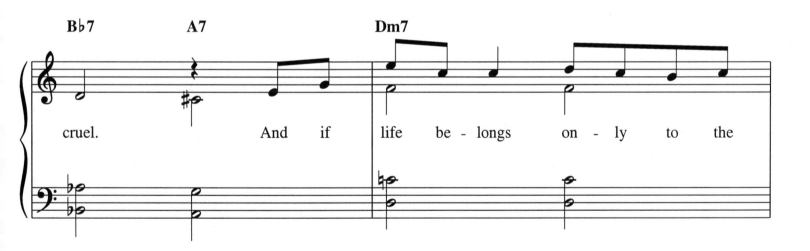

Bb7   A7   Dm7

cruel. And if life be - longs on - ly to the

Em7   Am7   Dm7   F/G   Cdim7

strong, Al - fie, _____ what will you lend on an old gold - en rule? As

cresc.

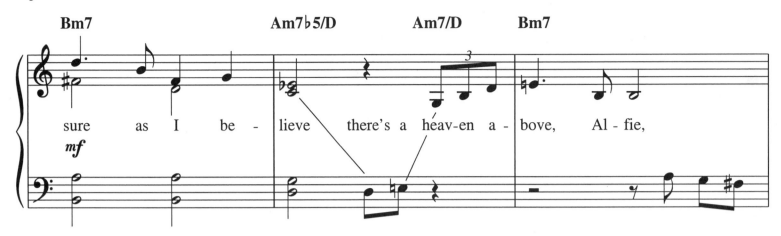

sure as I be - lieve there's a heav-en a - bove, Al - fie,

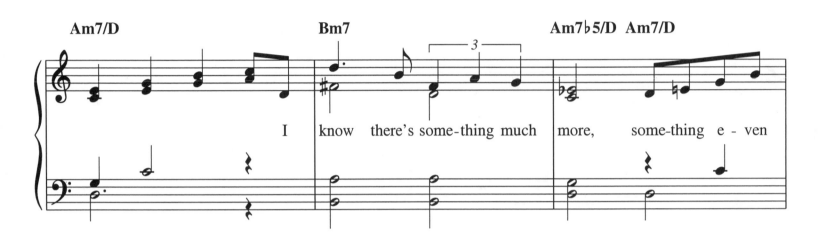

I know there's some-thing much more, some-thing e - ven

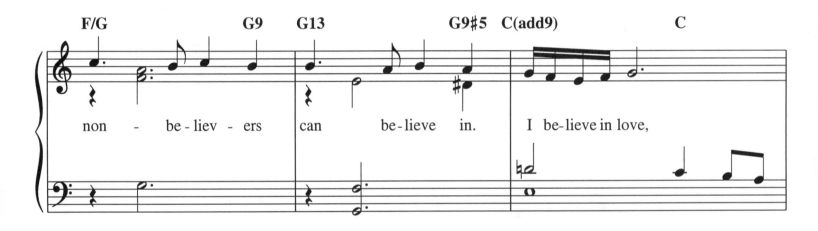

non - be - liev - ers can be - lieve in. I be-lieve in love,

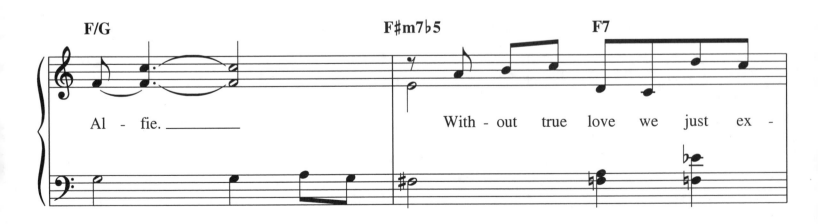

Al - fie. _____ With - out true love we just ex -

(They Long to Be)
CLOSE TO YOU

Lyric by HAL DAVID
Music by BURT BACHARACH

Slowly with a steady beat

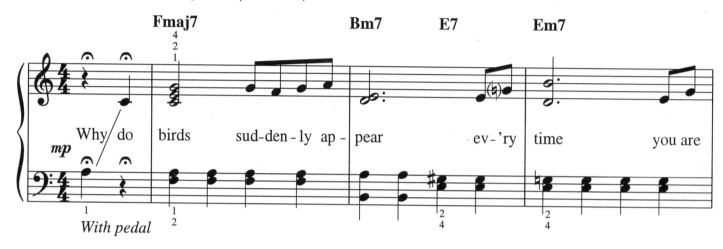

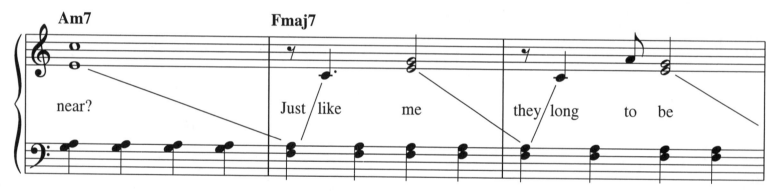

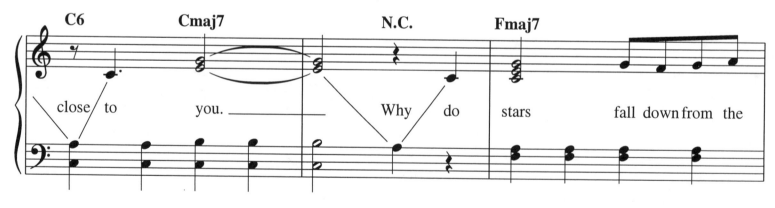

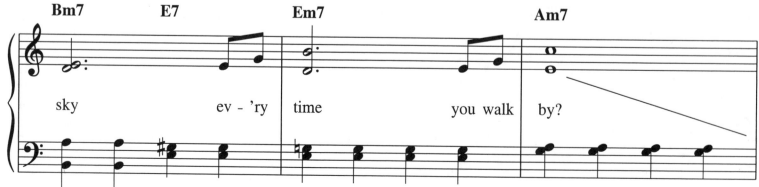

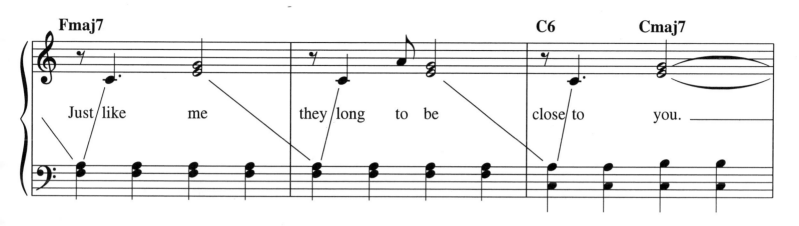

Just like me they long to be close to you. _____

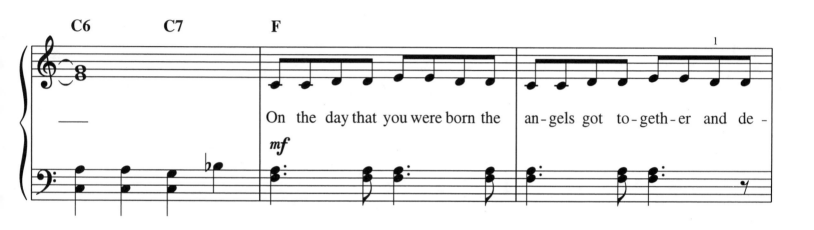

_____ On the day that you were born the an-gels got to-geth-er and de-

cid-ed to cre-ate a dream come true. So, they sprink-led moon dust in your hair of

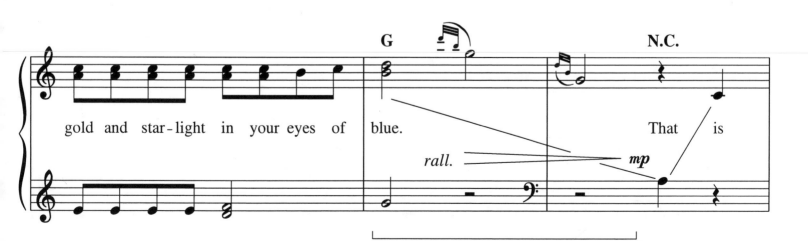

gold and star-light in your eyes of blue. That is

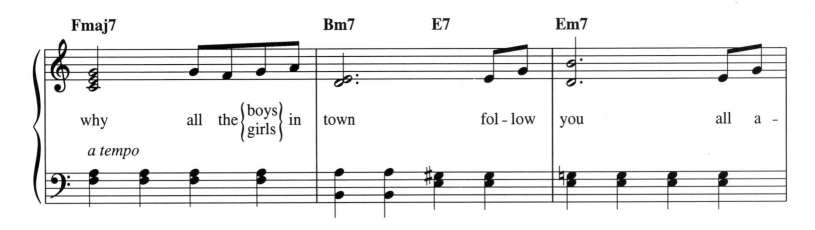

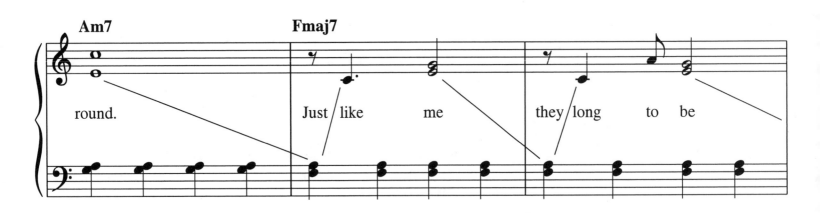

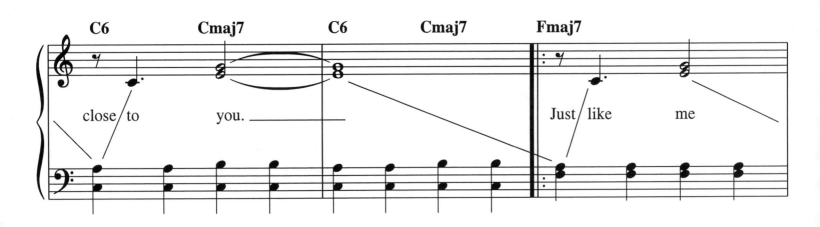

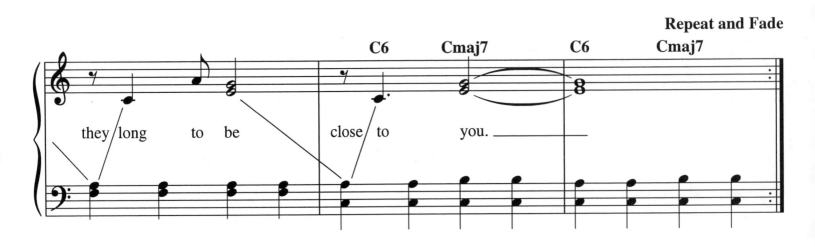

I'LL NEVER FALL IN LOVE AGAIN

from PROMISES, PROMISES

Lyric by HAL DAVID
Music by BURT BACHARACH

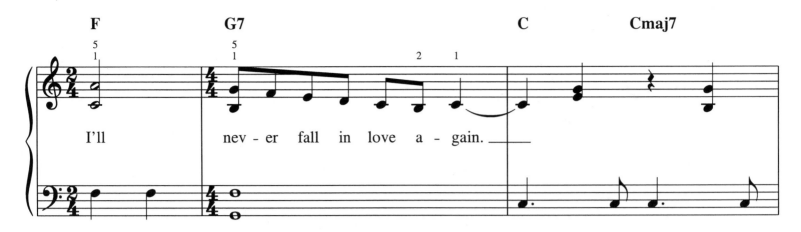

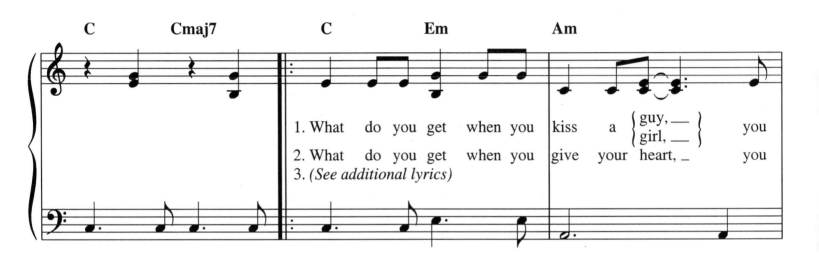

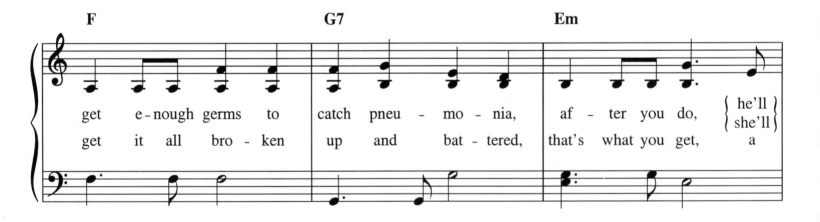

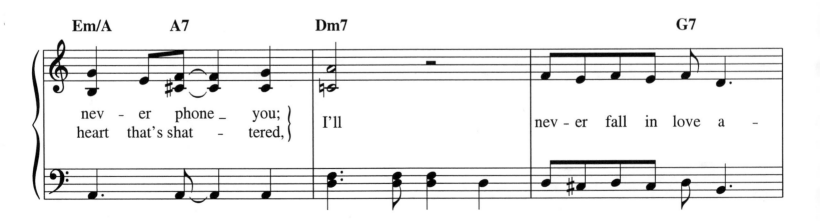

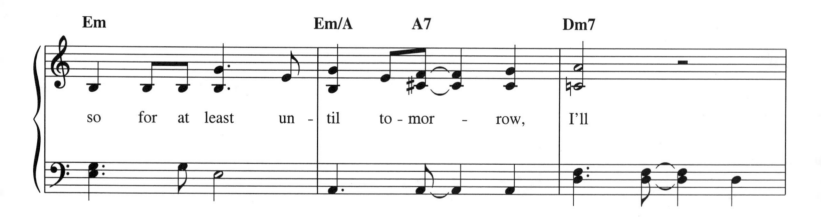

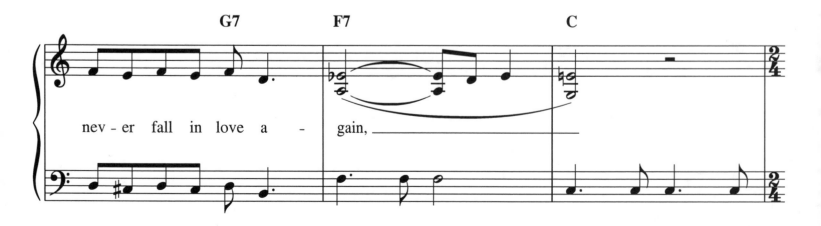

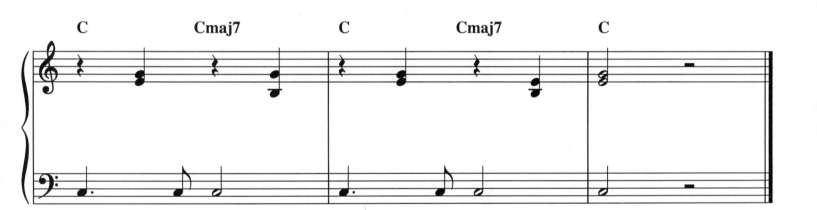

Additional Lyrics

3. What do you get when you need a { guy, }
                                     { girl, }
   You get enough tears to fill an ocean,
   That's what you get for all your devotion;
   I'll never fall in love again,
   I'll never fall in love again.
   Chorus

DO YOU KNOW THE WAY TO SAN JOSE

Lyric by HAL DAVID
Music by BURT BACHARACH

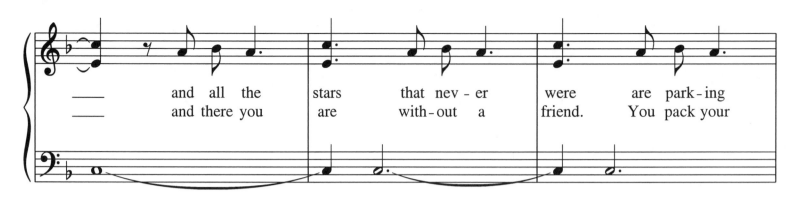

and all the stars that nev - er were are park - ing
and there you are with - out a friend. You pack your

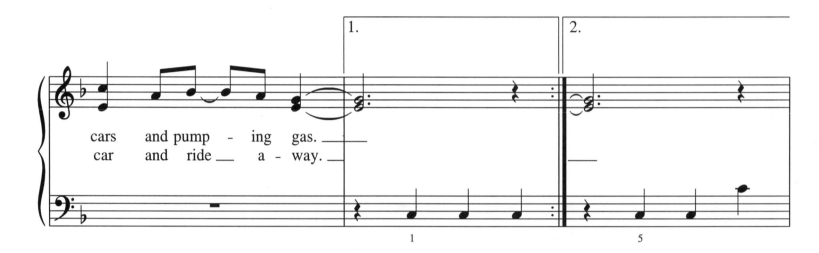

cars and pump - ing gas.
car and ride __ a - way.

F **Bb6** **F**

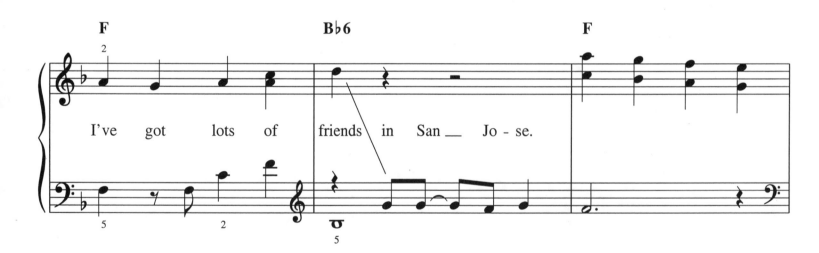

I've got lots of friends in San __ Jo - se.

Bb6

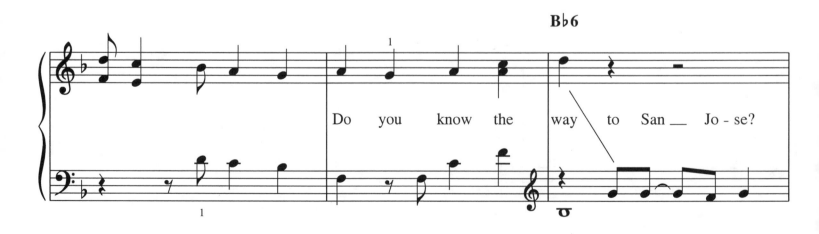

Do you know the way to San __ Jo - se?

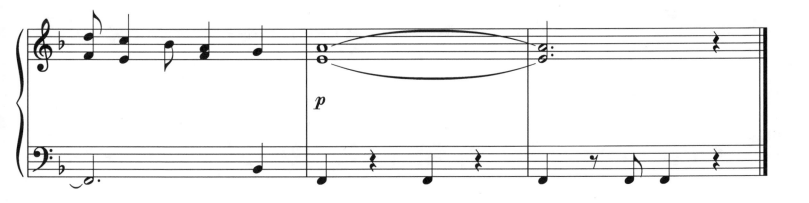

DON'T MAKE ME OVER

Lyric by HAL DAVID
Music by BURT BACHARACH

Rock Ballad

Don't make me o - ver, ____
Don't make me o - ver, ____
now that I can't make it with - out you.
now that I'd do an - y - thing for you.

Don't make me o - ver, ____
Don't make me o - ver, ____
I would - n't
now that you

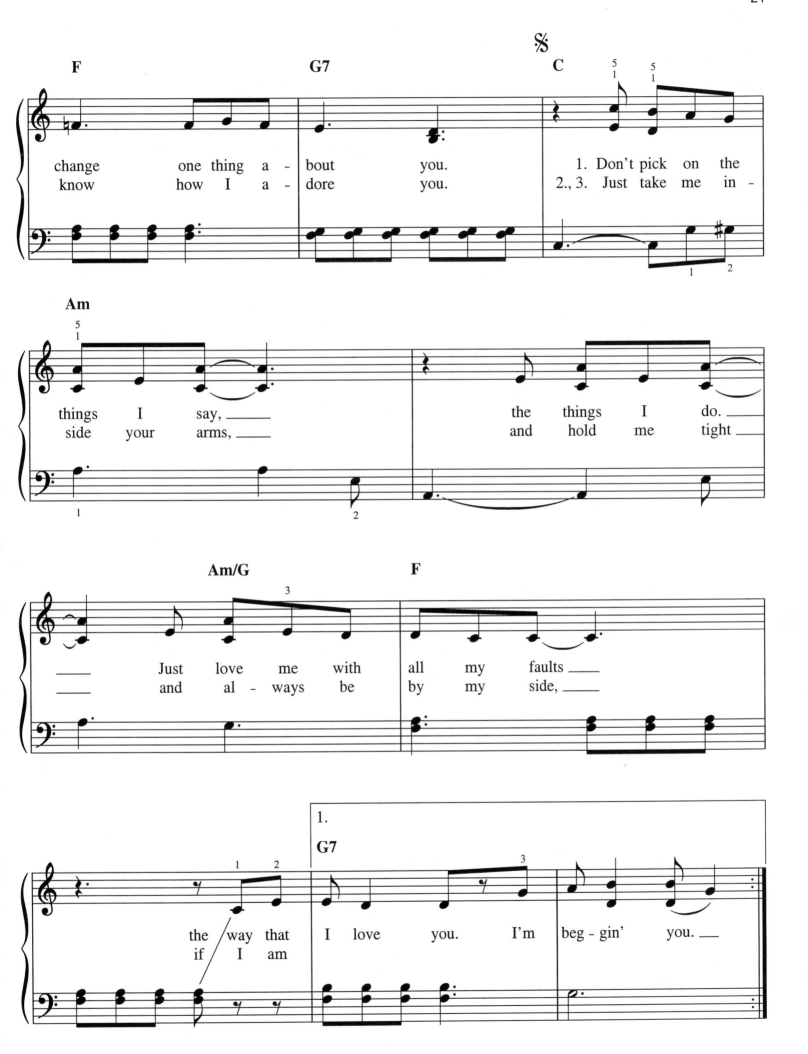

D.S. al Coda

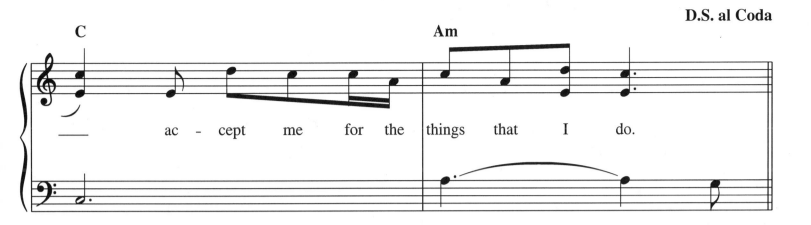

ac - cept me for the things that I do.

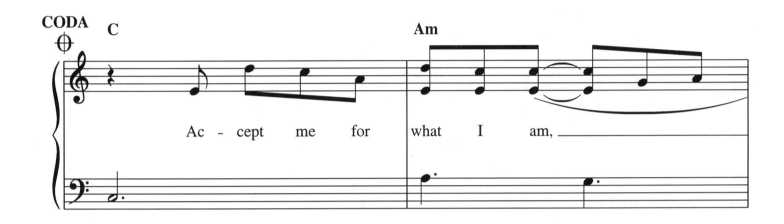

CODA

Ac - cept me for what I am, _____

ac - cept me for the things that I do. *gradually softer*

rit. *p*

A HOUSE IS NOT A HOME

Lyric by HAL DAVID
Music by BURT BACHARACH

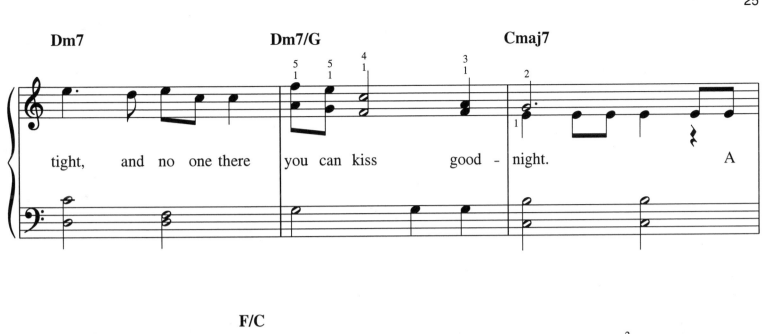

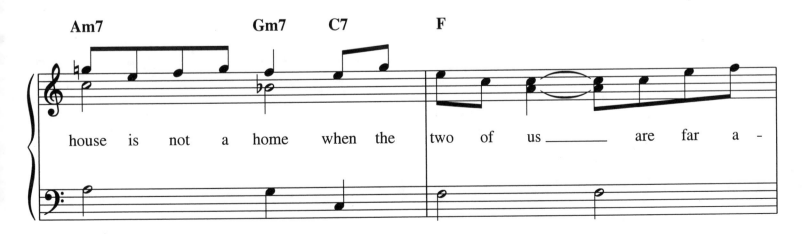

I SAY A LITTLE PRAYER

Lyric by HAL DAVID
Music by BURT BACHARACH

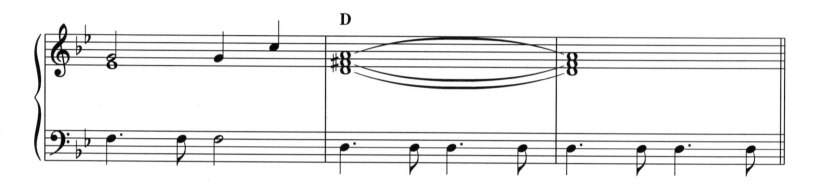

The mo-ment I wake up, before I put
I run for the bus, dear, while rid-ing I

on my make-up _____ I say a lit-tle prayer for
think of us, dear. _____ I say a lit-tle prayer for

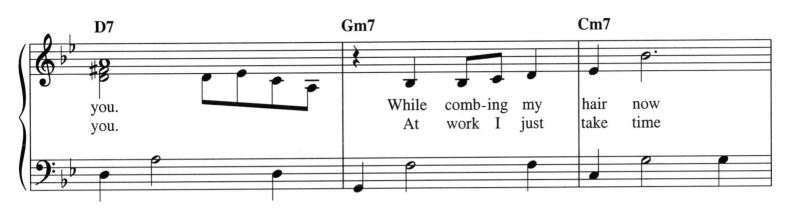

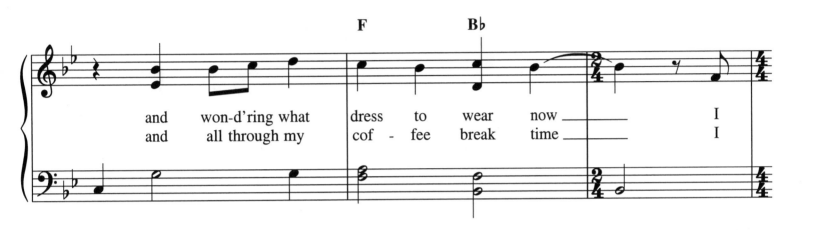

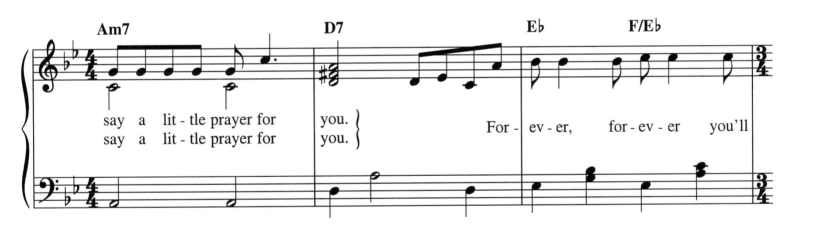

nev - er will part. Oh, how I'll love you. To - geth-er, to - geth-er, that's

how it must be. To live with - out you would on - ly mean heart-break for

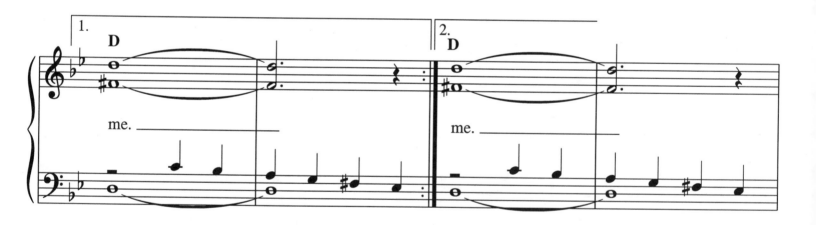

me. _____ me. _____

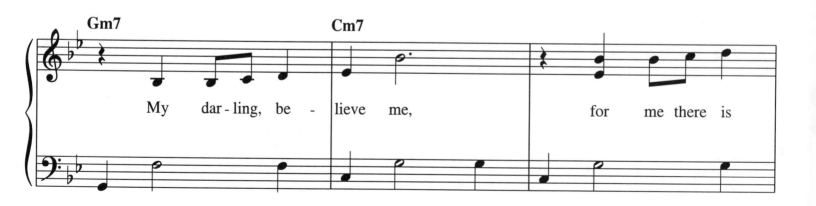

My dar - ling, be - lieve me, for me there is

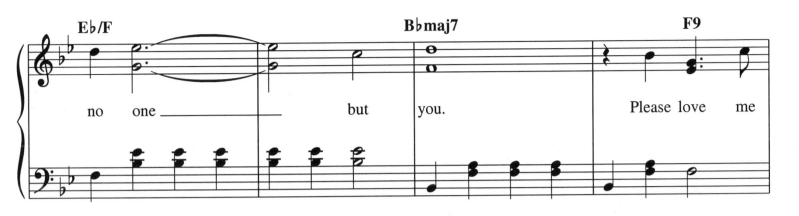

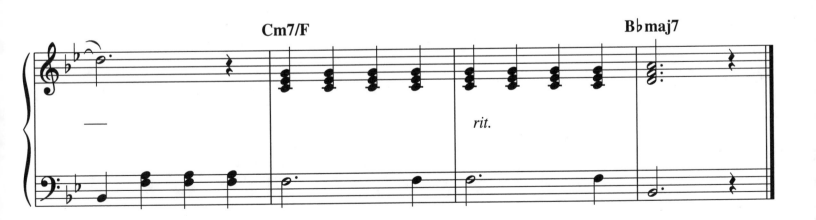

THE LOOK OF LOVE

from CASINO ROYALE

Words by HAL DAVID
Music by BURT BACHARACH

look   of   love,   it's say - ing
mine   to -   night,   let this be

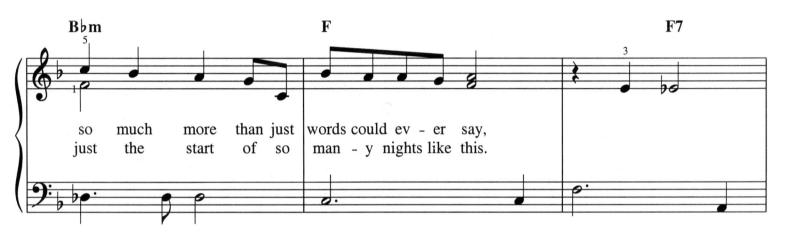

so   much   more   than just | words could ev - er say,
just   the   start   of   so | man - y nights like this.

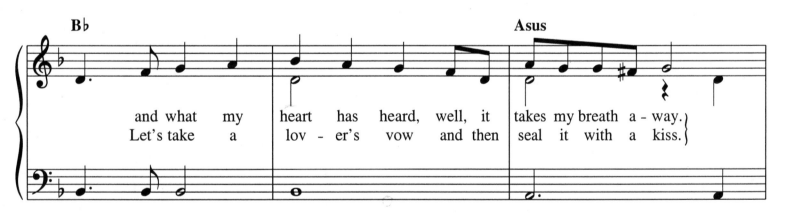

and what   my | heart has   heard, well, it | takes my breath a - way.
Let's take a | lov - er's vow   and then | seal it with a kiss.

I can   hard - ly wait to hold you, feel ___ my arms a - round you,

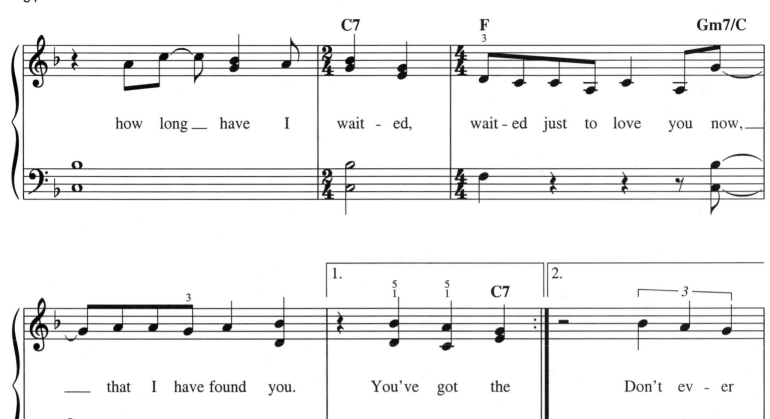

MAGIC MOMENTS

Lyric by HAL DAVID
Music by BURT BACHARACH

Slow Shuffle

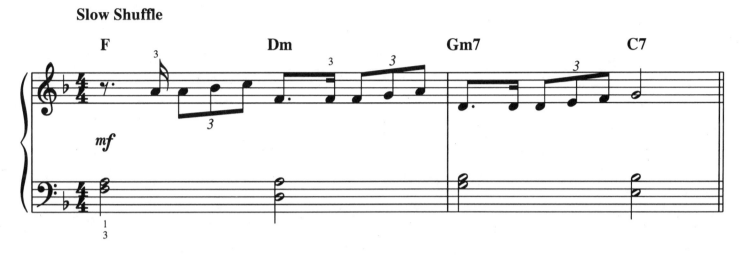

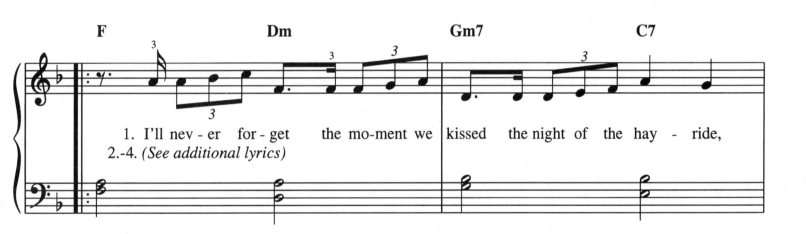

1. I'll nev-er for-get the mo-ment we kissed the night of the hay-ride,
2.-4. *(See additional lyrics)*

the way that we hugged to try to keep warm while tak-ing a sleigh-ride.

Chorus

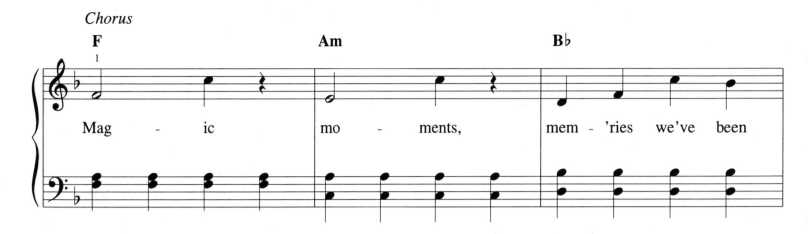

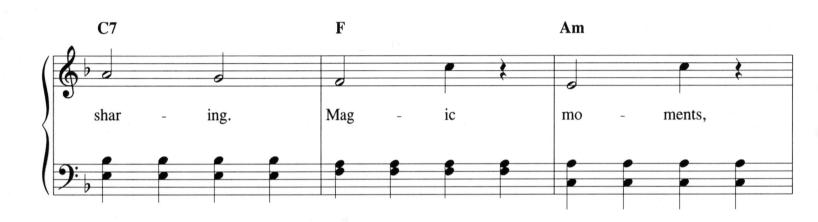

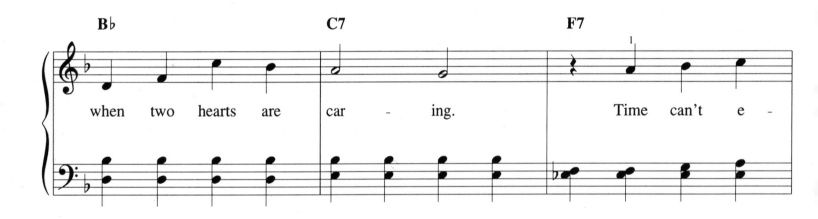

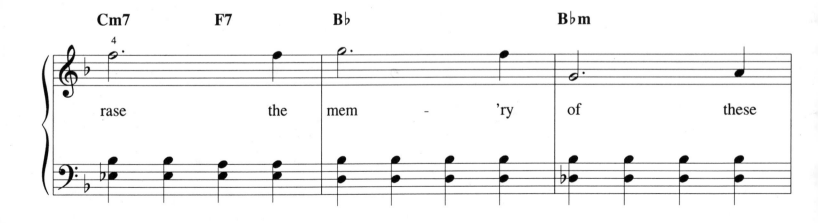

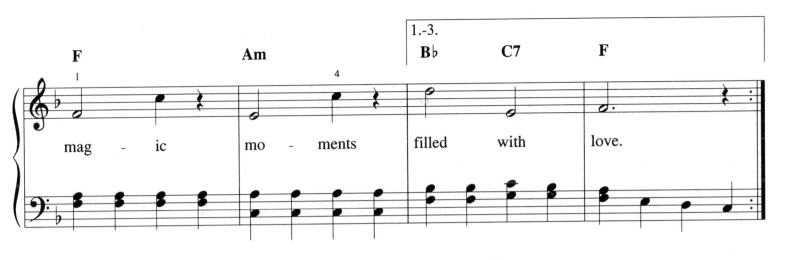

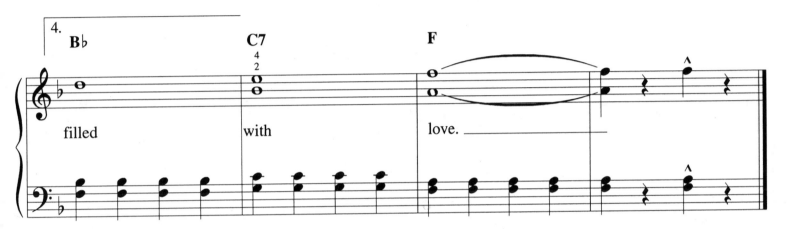

Additional Lyrics

2. The telephone call that tied up the line for hours and hours,
   The Saturday dance { I / you } got up the nerve to send { you / me } some flowers.
   To Chorus

3. The way that we cheered whenever our team was scoring a touchdown,
   The time that the floor fell out of { my / your } car when { I / you } put the clutch down.
   To Chorus

4. The penny arcade, the games that we played, the fun and the prizes,
   The Halloween Hop when everyone came in funny disguises.
   To Chorus

MAKE IT EASY ON YOURSELF

Lyric by HAL DAVID
Music by BURT BACHARACH

so ver - y hard to do.

And

if the way I hold you

can't com - pare to { his } ca -
{ her }

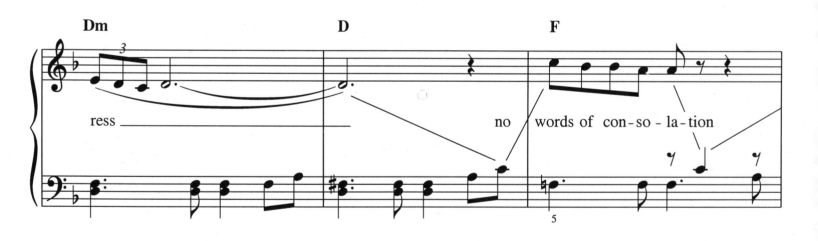

ress _____

no words of con - so - la - tion

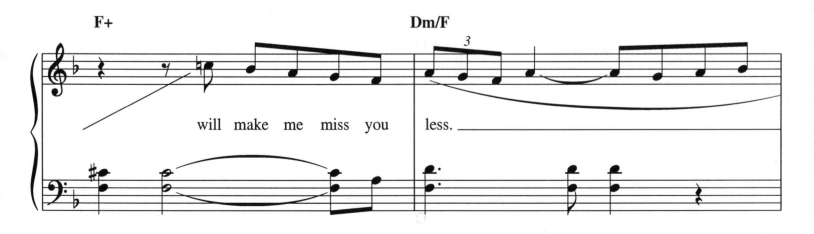

will make me miss you

less. _____

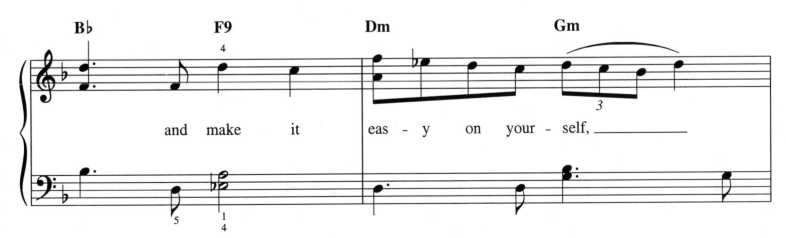

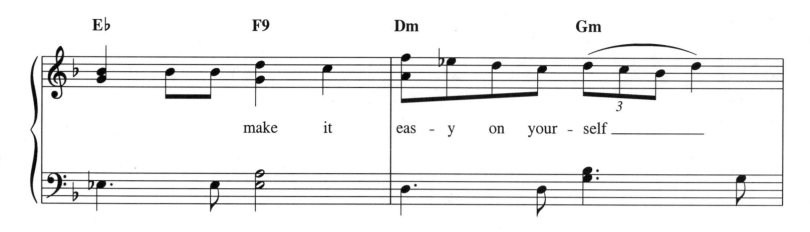

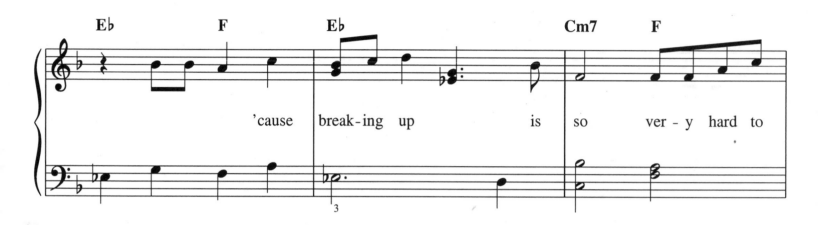

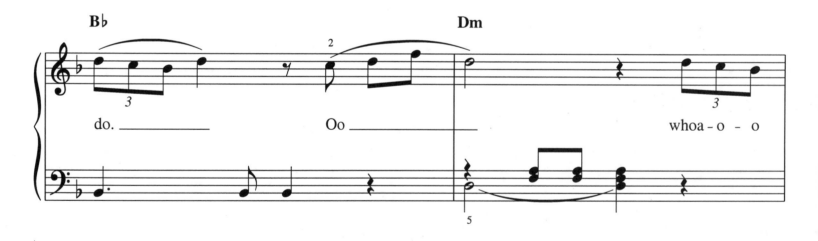

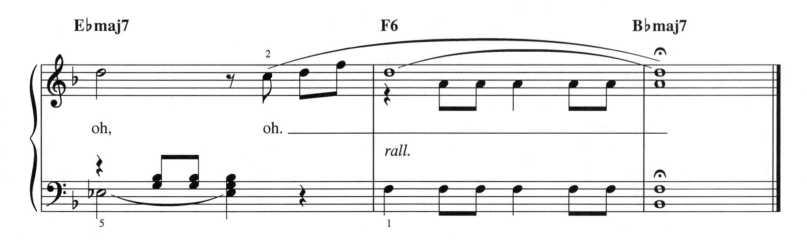

WHAT THE WORLD NEEDS NOW IS LOVE

Lyric by HAL DAVID
Music by BURT BACHARACH

love, sweet love. No, not just for some,_____ but for

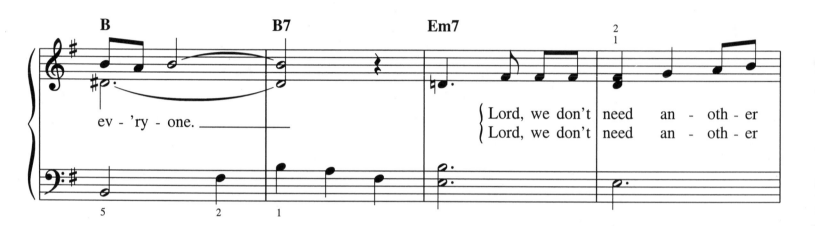

ev - 'ry - one. _____

Lord, we don't need an - oth - er
Lord, we don't need an - oth - er

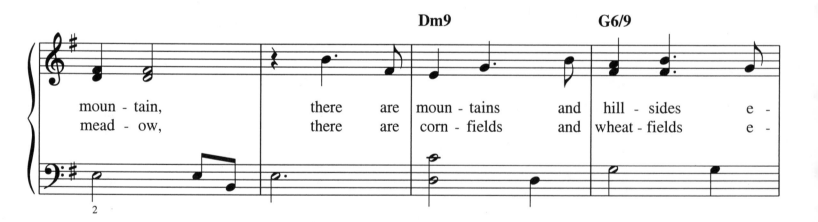

moun - tain, there are moun - tains and hill - sides e -
mead - ow, there are corn - fields and wheat - fields e -

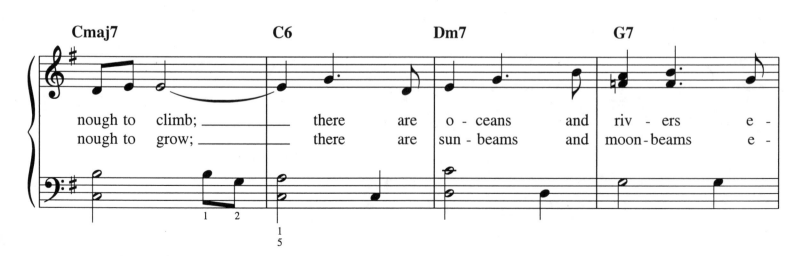

nough to climb; _____ there are o - ceans and riv - ers e -
nough to grow; _____ there are sun - beams and moon-beams e -

ONE LESS BELL TO ANSWER

Lyric by HAL DAVID
Music by BURT BACHARACH

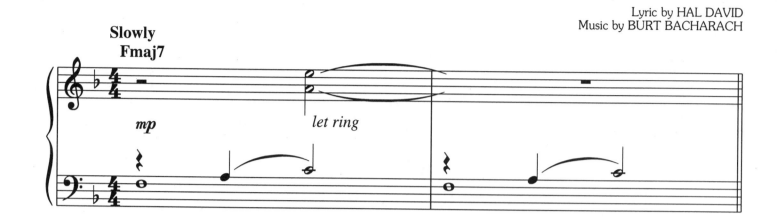

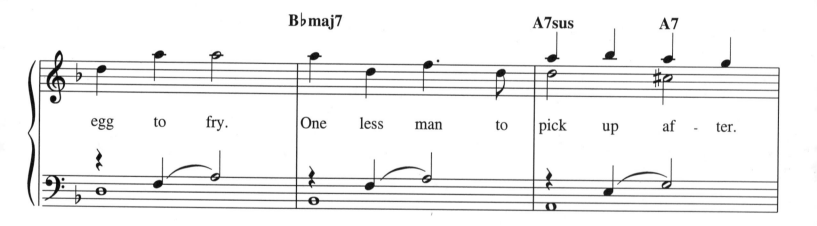

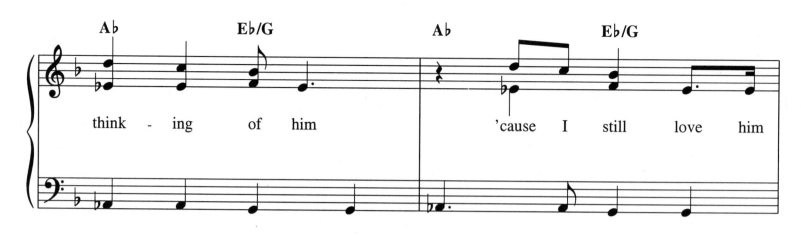

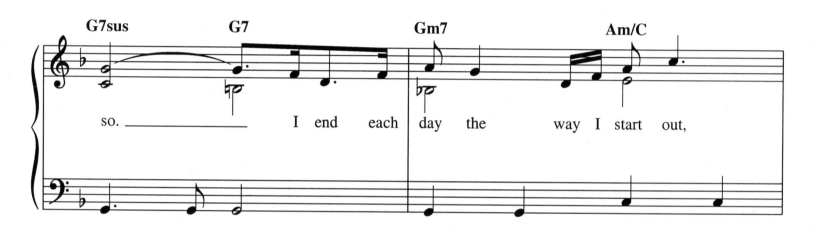

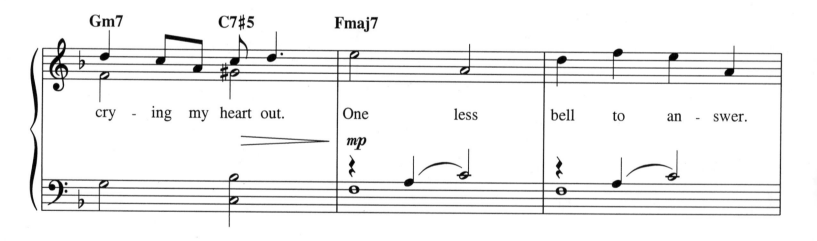

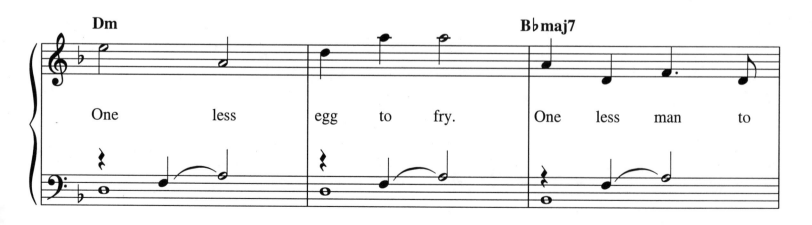

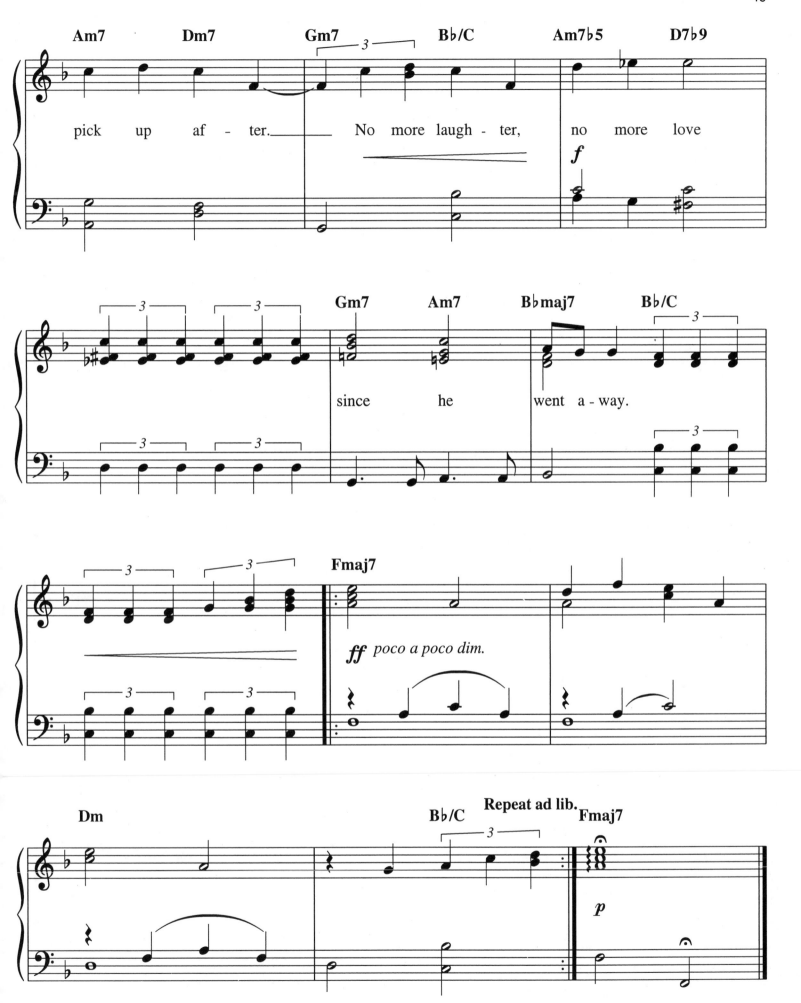

RAINDROPS KEEP FALLIN' ON MY HEAD

Lyric by HAL DAVID
Music by BURT BACHARACH

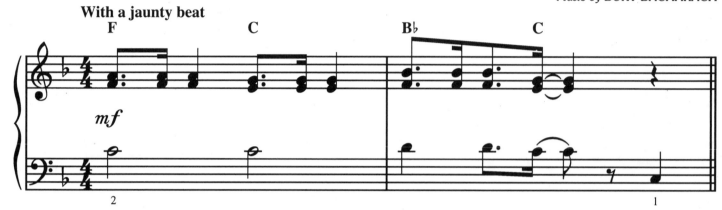

Rain - drops keep fall - in' on my head, and
did me some talk - in' to the sun. And

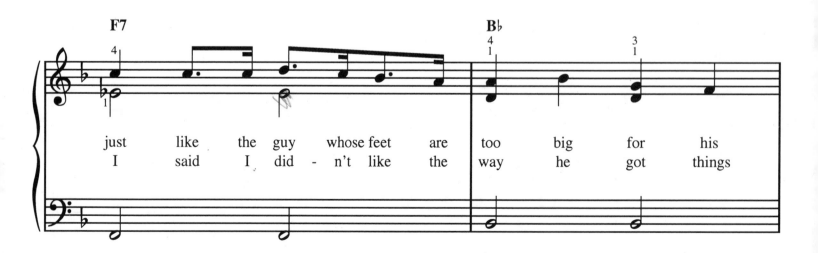

just like the guy whose feet are too big for his
I said I did – n't like the way he got things

feat me.   It   won't be   long till   hap - pi - ness steps

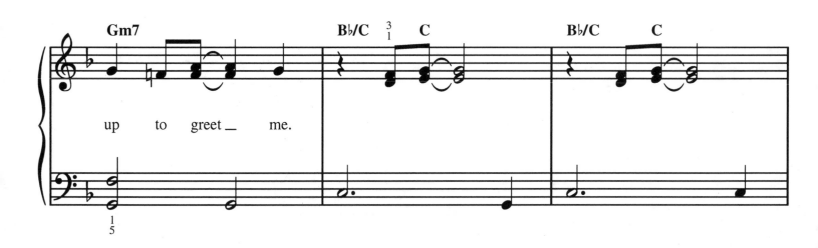

up   to   greet _ me.

Rain - drops keep fall - in' on my   head,   but

that   does - n't mean my eyes   will   soon   be   turn - in'

red.   Cry - in's not for me   'cause

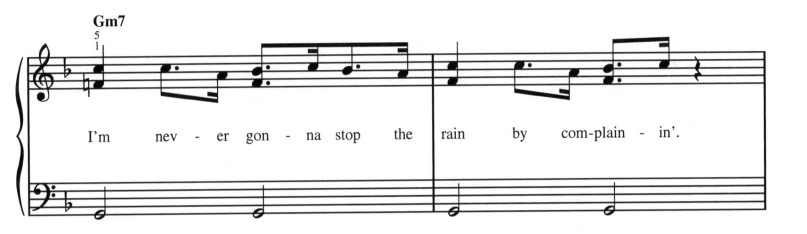

I'm nev - er gon - na stop the rain by com-plain - in'.

Be - cause I'm   free,

noth - in's wor - ry - in'   me. _____

THIS GUY'S IN LOVE WITH YOU

Lyric by HAL DAVID
Music by BURT BACHARACH

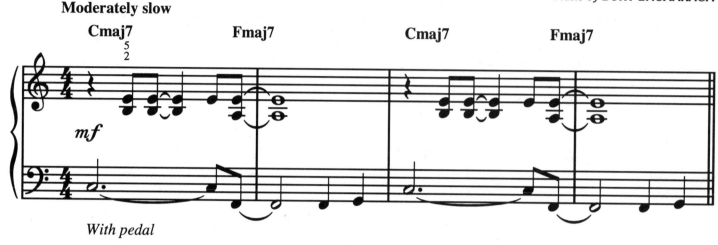

You see ___ this guy, ___ this guy's in love with you.

— Yes, I'm ___ in love. ___ Who

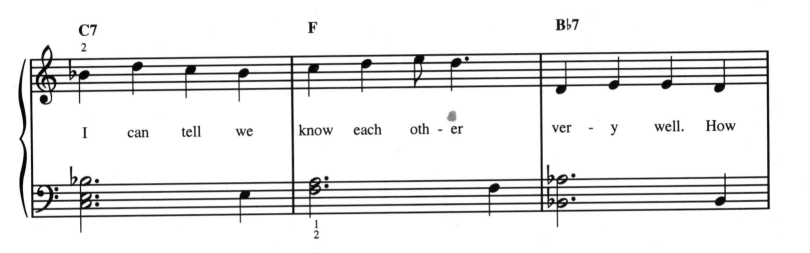

let my heart keep break-ing, 'cause I need __ your love. __

__ I want __ your love. __ __

Say you're __ in love, in love with this

guy. __ If not, I'll just die. __

rit.

WALK ON BY

Lyric by HAL DAVID
Music by BURT BACHARACH

WISHIN' AND HOPIN'

Lyric by HAL DAVID
Music by BURT BACHARACH

Moderately

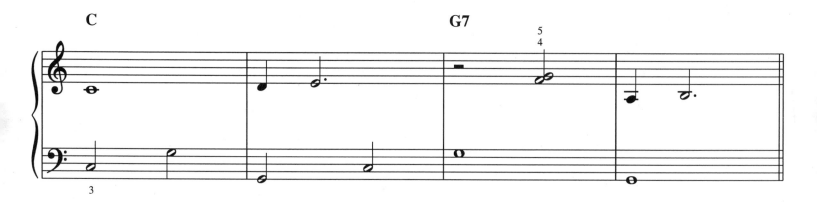

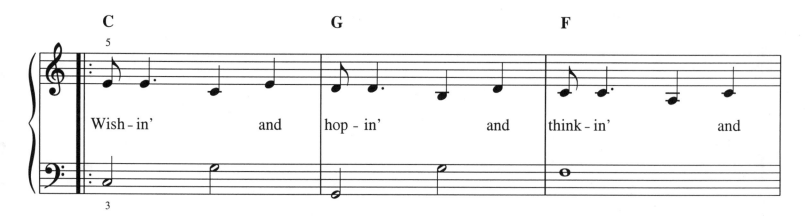

Wish - in' and hop - in' and think - in' and

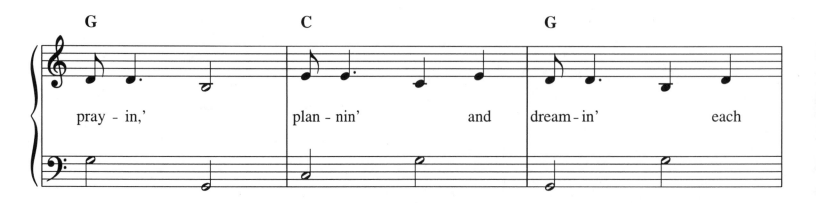

pray - in,' plan - nin' and dream - in' each

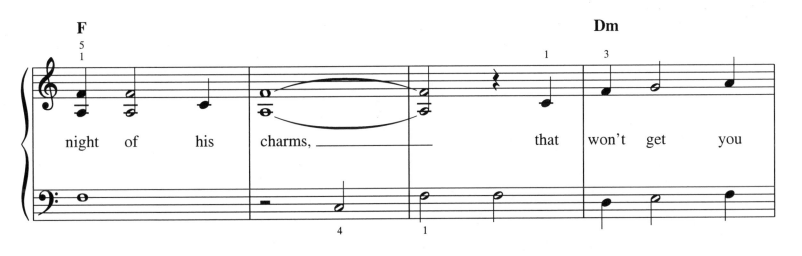

night of his charms, _____ that won't get you

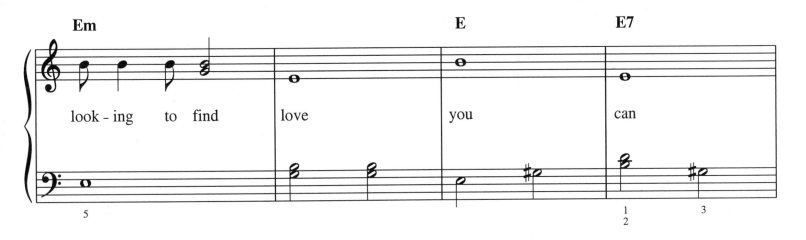

in - to his arms. So if you're

look - ing to find love you can

share. _____ All you got - ta do is

hold him   and   kiss him,   and   love him   and

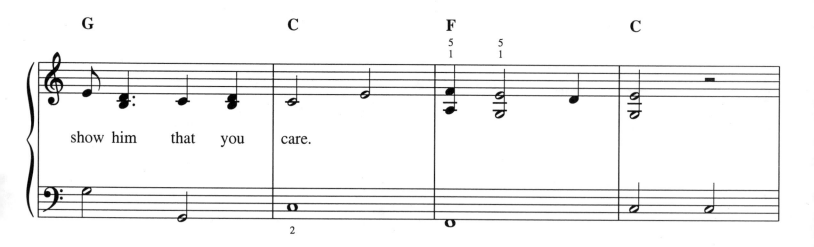

show him   that   you   care.

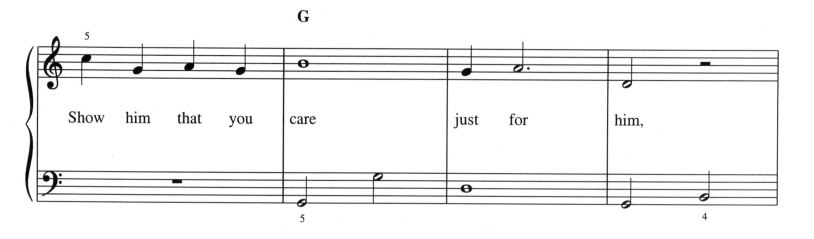

Show   him   that   you   care   just   for   him,

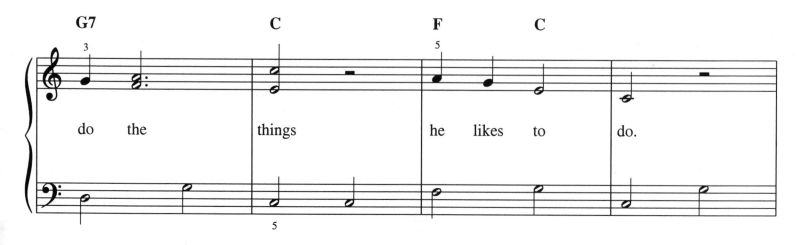

do   the   things   he   likes   to   do.

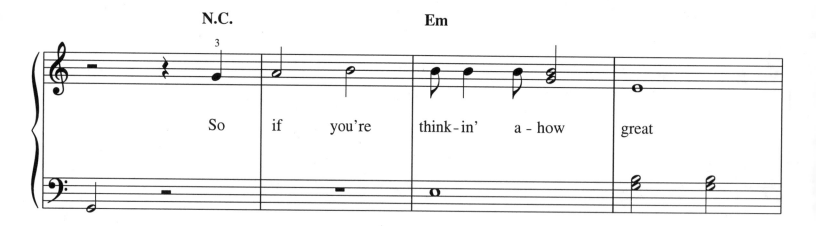

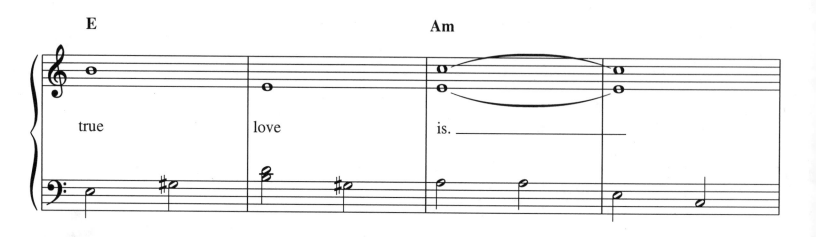

WIVES AND LOVERS
(Hey, Little Girl)
from the Paramount Picture WIVES AND LOVERS

Words by HAL DAVID
Music by BURT BACHARACH

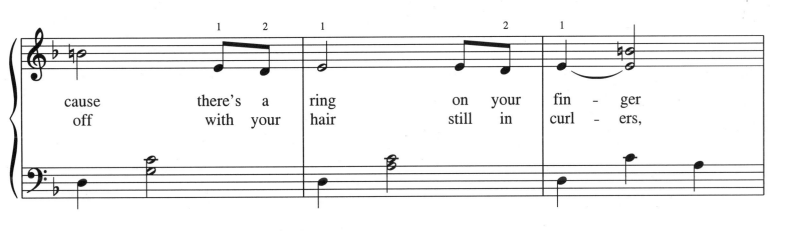

cause there's a ring on your fin - ger
off with your hair still in curl - ers,

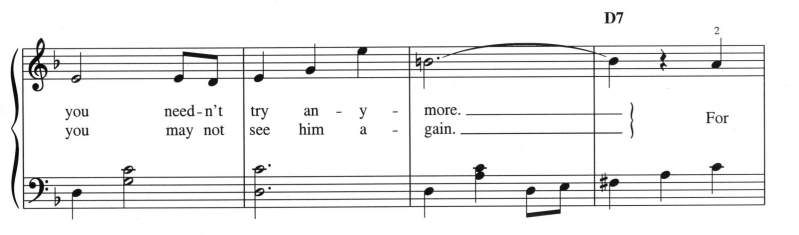

you need-n't try an - y - more. _____ For
you may not see him a - gain. _____

wives should al - ways be lov - ers too.

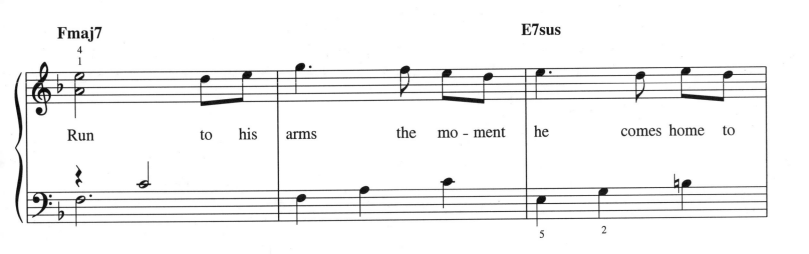

Run to his arms the mo - ment he comes home to

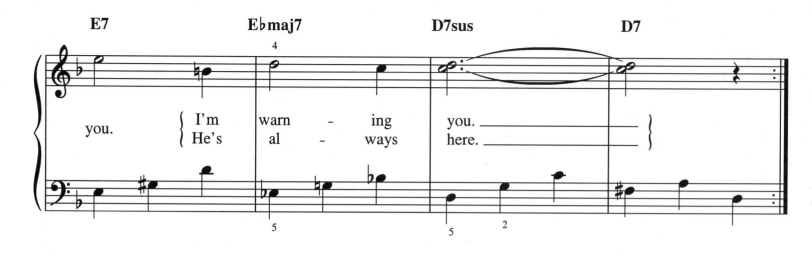

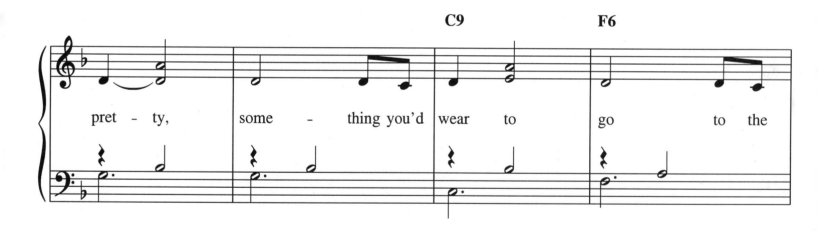

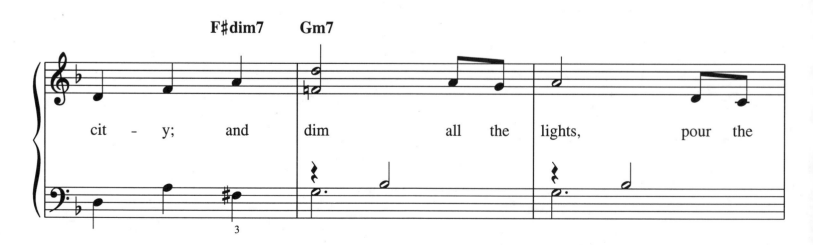

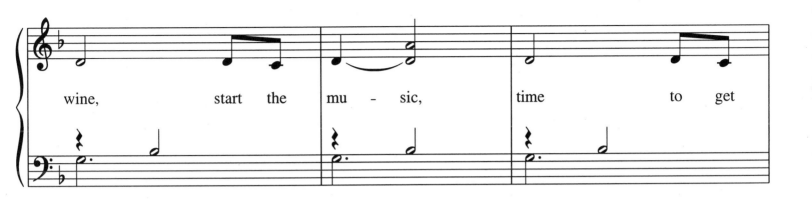

wine,   start the mu – sic,   time   to get

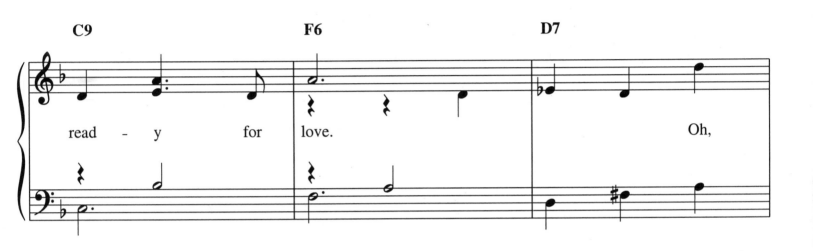

C9   **F6**   **D7**

read – y for love.   Oh,

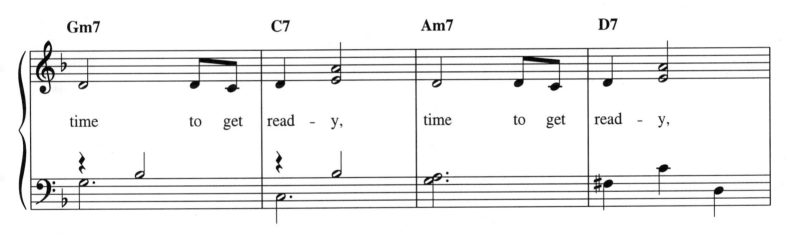

Gm7   **C7**   **Am7**   **D7**

time   to get read – y,   time   to get read – y,

Gm7   **C7**   **F6**

time   to get read – y for love.

rit.

5